G000273924

HOUNSLOW AS IT WAS

A selection of photographs with captions

of

Hounslow, Cranford, Heston & Isleworth

by

The Hounslow & District History Society

Cover Subjects: Front, top left: High Street, Hounslow c.1884, looking towards the Bell junction and Neal's Corner. The Printing Office was run by the Gotelee family from 1837-1917. After which it was continued until the 1960's by A. Maddison and Son. Bottom left: St. Leonard's Church, Heston, c.1900–1910, viewed from New Heston Road, showing the 14th century tower with the body of the church rebuilt 1866. An animal pound was to be found on the triangular green to the left. Bottom right: The London Apprentice and the Isleworth riverside c.1900–1905, showing the London Apprentice before the bay window on the first floor below the inn's name was added c.1906. The granary store to Kidd's Mill can be seen to the left. Top right: Cranford House and St. Dunstan's Church at the end of the 19th century. The only part of Cranford House to remain today is the stable block which can be seen between the trees and the tower of the church. Back cover: Hounslow High Street, c.1910–1915, showing the Middlesex Chronicle office, which moved to a site opposite in 1939. To the right can be seen A. Jeffs, leather shop, which along with the two shops to its right was purchased by Marks and Spensers about 1930.

First edition May 1977
Second impression November 1980
Third impression May 1981

Published by Hendon Publishing Co. Ltd., Hendon Mill, Nelson, Lancashire
Text © The Hounslow & District History Society, 1977.
Printed by: Fretwell & Brian Ltd., Howden Hall, Silsden, Keighley, Yorks.

HENDON
£2.40

Introduction

This book attempts to show the town of Hounslow and the villages of Heston, Isleworth, and Cranford from the time they were first united for local governemnt purposes in 1875 as the Urban Sanitary District of Heston and Isleworth, to the end of the 1920's, prior to the formation of the Borough of Heston and Isleworth in 1932.

Most of the photographs show the area at the end of the 19th century and the early 20th century up to the First World War. This period saw the growth and development of the town of Hounslow to a position of prominence within the area for the first time in its history, and the villages of Cranford, Heston, and Isleworth in their final years as independent, rural, agricultural villages which had changed very slowly over the centuries.

The photographs for each area have been kept together in an attempt to give an overall picture of each community during the period. The book ends at the close of the 1920's when the explosion of urban development in the London suburbs was about to begin, heralding the destruction of the area as a place of character and rural charm. This development increased at an alarming rate throughout the 1930's, ceased during the Second World War, but continued apace in the 1960's, until today areas such as Hounslow High Street and the village of Cranford bear no resemblence to the photographs in the book.

The Hounslow and District History Society, formed in 1960, tries with varying degrees of success to ensure that the few remaining buildings of the 18th, 19th, and earlier centuries remain for posterity. Today most of the fields and farms have disappeared, and the only open spaces are provided by the local authority parks, and the much diminished estates of Osterley Park and Syon House.

It is hoped that the book will revive memories for people who have known the area for many years, and also show newcomers how attractive this part of South West Middlesex used to be.

Acknowledgements: The Hounslow and District History Society wishes to thank Hounslow Public Library for permission to reproduce the photographs, which all came from the Library's Local History Collection. Also "The Middlesex Chronicle" whose volumes provided much of the information for dating and locating the photographs accurately.

The photographs were selected and the descriptions written by Gillian Morris and Andrea Cameron with help from Susan Higlett, Tom White, and Francis Clive-Ross.

1. Below: The Bell Inn, Hounslow, c.1899, shortly before it was pulled down and the present building erected in 1900. The Bell is one of the most well-known landmarks in Hounslow, and one of its oldest named inns. It served the traffic of the coaching era from c. 1750–1850. Until the 19th century, The Bell looked out onto Hounslow Heath and the gibbets lining the edge of the Staines Road, where the bodies of criminals were hung in chains. In 1802 three men called Haggerty, Hollaway, and Hansfield travelled from London to The Bell Inn, where they sat drinking and planning to murder Mr. Steele, a lavender vendor, who travelled from London to his nursery at Feltham. The murder took place by the 11th mile post on the Staines Road. They were not caught, tried, and found guilty until 1807, when they were hanged.

Staines Road and The Heath . . .

2. Top left: The Hussar Public House, Staines Road, c. 1912. This was the tram terminus until 1921, when it was altered to the Bell Public House. In 1935, when the trolley buses replaced the trams, the Duke of Wellington Public House was made the terminus. The Hussar was rebuilt in 1933. The Light Horse, seen to the right of the Teas sign, and some of the shops, were demolished c. 1974. The area is opposite what remains of Hounslow Heath, and was known as a military neighbourhood because of the barracks, situated at the far end of the turning by the Hussar.

3. Bottom left: Hounslow Barracks, c. 1910. The barracks are situated in Beavers Lane. Prior to 1793 there were no barracks in Hounslow, although military encampments had been held on the Heath from 1685. In 1793 the government paid for the cavalry barracks to be built, and in 1818 the War Department purchased approximately 300 acres of Hounslow Heath as a training ground for the cavalry. 1875 saw the addition of a large infantry barracks.

4. Right: The first flight from England to Australia took off from Hounslow Heath on November 12th 1919, and arrived at Port Darwin, Australia, on December 10th 1919, having completed the flight in 27 days, 20 hours, 20 minutes. The aeroplane, seen in the photograph prior to take-off, was a Vickers "Vimy". Part of Hounslow Heath was an airfield during the First World War, used by the Royal Flying Corps. In 1919 it was used for commercial purposes such as the first service between London and Paris, but in 1920 the airport was transferred to Croydon.

5. Left: Heston Flour Mill was built on Hounslow Heath, north of the Staines Road, after the Enclosure Act 1818. It was used to grind corn. A steam engine was added in a near-by building about 1891. All the buildings were destroyed by fire on August 24th 1895. Parke-Davis and Co. Ltd. later took over the site and built a factory, which they used until they left Hounslow for Wales in 1972.

6. Top right: Tram at the Hounslow ("Bell") terminus soon after the opening of the extension of the line from Kew Bridge in 1901. The drinking fountain was removed in 1904, when the public lavatories were built.

7. Bottom right: Holy Trinity Church, c. 1910, was built in 1828 on the site of Hounslow Chapel, which was the only part of the Priory of Holy Trinity to remain after the Dissolution of the Monasteries by Henry VIII. The church was known as Hounslow Chapel after the opening in 1829 until 1856, when the parish of Holy Trinity was created by the passing of an Act of Parliament. A chancel was added in 1855, and the church reseated in 1880. On the 1st June 1943 the church was gutted by fire; not from any action of the Second World War, but by two schoolboys setting fire to it. A restoration fund was started, but the only way enough money could be raised, was by pulling down the remains of the church, and selling off part of the churchyard for building development. This was done in 1959, and the new church was consecrated in 1963.

8. Left: Hounslow High Street in 1899, showing Treaty House just before it was demolished, in order to widen the High Street to accommodate the tramway from Isleworth to Hounslow. It is not known how old the house was, nor why it was so named. Parts of the house were described as "very old", and the chestnut tree in the grounds was said to be over 300 years old.

9. Right: The garden of Treaty House stood on the site of the present Barclays Bank at the corner of Treaty Road. On the extreme left of the photograph can be seen Dr. J. A. Douglas, and next to him his assistant, Dr. Hayworth. In 1900 Treaty House was demolished by the Heston and Isleworth District Council, who cut Treaty Road, and built the Town Hall, Swimming Baths, and Hounslow Public Library, between 1903 and 1905.

10. Top left: Hounslow High Street, c. 1870. On the left is the first Town Hall built 1858–1859, and used until the Treaty Road building opened in 1904. It then became the Empire Cinema until demolished in 1954. Waitrose Supermarket now stands on the site. On the right can be seen the Nag's Head Public House, demolished in 1954, and thought to be the oldest inn in Hounslow. The building was about 350 years old. In the distance on the right, can be seen the inn signs for The Old Ship, and The Red Lion. On the left, opposite The Red Lion, can be seen Treaty House.

11. Bottom left: Horne's the estate agent, c. 1903. This is the oldest business in Hounslow High Street, having been founded by John Peisley in 1803. The business has been carried on at the same site, and by the same family, since its formation. In 1887 John Horne took over the business from his uncle John Peisley. The shop front was altered in 1909, and 1932, but much of the original building still remains. To the left can be seen Shackleton's the drapers, and to the right Warren Brothers, another draper's shop.

12. Right: Hounslow Post Office 1893, situated at the western end of an early 19th century building called Oak House. This building, much altered, was later the premises of the Middlesex Chronicle. The head post office for Hounslow was here from 1807–1897, when it moved to the corner of Holloway Street, opposite The Lion and Lamb. In 1932 it moved to its present premises in Holloway Street. From 1807 until 1916 the post office was in the charge of the Butler family, commencing with Miss Ann Butler 1807–1847, and followed by Mr. Edward Butler 1847–1860. The three successive postmistresses were all Misses Butler.

13. Left: Robert Bates had a leather shop here in 1874, and across the road his brother, 'Miser Bates', had another shop. Next door, on the right, can be seen the barber's pole of Doves, the barber, where a shave could be had for one penny. To the right can be seen the edge of a forge, run by Tom Broughton, a vet. The site is about where The Midland Bank now stands.

14. Left: Queen Victoria's Diamond Jubilee, June 22nd 1897. The photograph shows the troops in Hounslow High Street on their return from the London Celebrations. They were encamped on Hounslow Heath for the period of the Jubilee, and attracted thousands of sightseers to watch them march through Hounslow. They included squadrons of the Hussars, the Dragoon Guards, the Lancers, the Royal Artillery, and the New South Wales Mounted Rifles. On the left of the photograph is the clock which hung outside Paul Mecklenberg, a jeweller's shop, and was later purchased by Platt's Stores, and transferred across the road to their premises. On the right is Henry Perks's large drapery store, now the site of British Home Stores.

15. Left: Hounslow High Street in the 1890s, looking towards the Broadway. On the left is H. Branson, men's outfitters, established in 1885. He was known as the 'shirt king'. The name is retained today although the family no longer own the shop. The Crown and Cushion Public House closed about 1900, and beyond it The Marquis of Granby, closed in 1906, and the licence was transferred to a new building at Southall. The site is now the western end of the C. & A. Store. On the right can be seen the shop of Edwin Stevens, basket maker. The tall building was known as Eagle Chambers where Mr. Bell, the watchmaker, lived. These buildings were demolished just before the Second World War.

16. Left: School House, situated at the junction of School Road with the High Street, was demolished in 1945. It opened in 1831 as The Hounslow Subscription School. The building was financially supported for many years by Mr. Henry Pownall, then living at Spring Grove House. At the beginning of this century the house was occupied by Mr. Duffy, a plumber and decorator. Later it was used as a store house by Binney's furniture dealers.

17. Left: The King's Arms, c. 1890, situated on the High Street, near to the junction with Kingsley Road, once called Kings Arms Lane. This building was rebuilt at the beginning of the century, and the replacement building demolished in 1973. The new public house is called The Chariot.

18. Left: Auntie Green's tobacconist 1890, with presumably Auntie Green in the doorway. Miss Maria Balloon Green was her correct name, and her shop was a popular haunt for cyclists touring clubs. She provided a shoulder to weep on for poor lads who were having a hard time. They would call in for a chat and a glass of lemonade. The shop later became Read and Hann, Corn Merchant, and was pulled down as part of the Broadway redevelopment in 1960. Matthews, a butcher's shop, now stands on this site.

19. Right: Hounslow Town Station opened on May 1st 1883, when the Metropolitan District Railway was extended to Hounslow, and stood on the site of the present bus garage. In 1886 the station closed, when the line was extended to Hounslow Barracks Station (now Hounslow West), but in 1903 the station reopened in competition to the trams, which came to Hounslow in 1901. It finally closed on May 1st 1909, when the new Hounslow Town Station opened on the site of the present Hounslow East Station, so named in 1925. This photograph was taken in 1905. The first bus garage opened on the site in 1913, and the present building in 1956.

20. Top left: Members of the Heston and Isleworth Local Board Fire Brigade with their first steam engine, c. 1889. The photograph was taken under the arches of the Hounslow Town Railway Station, now the site of the bus garage. The fire station had previously been in the Hanworth Road, at the rear of the premises now Giltrow's bakery. It later moved to the fire station in Montague Road. Seated on the right hand side of the fire engine is Mr. T. H. Emmett, who joined the local fire brigade in 1887, as a voluntary fireman. In 1890 he became a permanent fireman driver and steam man rising to Second Officer in 1911, and Chief Officer from 1925 until his retirement in 1933.

21. Bottom left: Kingsley Road in 1903. The two gentlemen are walking towards the High Street. On their left is Shaws Brown's farmhouse, which stood approximately at the turning to Taunton Avenue, and was demolished c. 1927. Kingsley Road was once called Kings Arms Lane.

22. Right: The Hounslow Omnibus c. 1860. The first record of a local omnibus service appeared in 1839 and stated: "Brunsden's Hounslow Omnibus leaves his house, the Bell Inn, every morning at nine o'clock, direct to the Bank, returning from St. Paul's Churchyard at 12 o'clock; it returns in the afternoon from the above Inn at $\frac{1}{4}$ before 4 o'clock to St. Paul's Churchyard from whence it returns at $\frac{1}{2}$ past 6" It is not known when the service to London ended; possibly when the underground railway came to Hounslow in 1883. Local horse buses between Kew and Hounslow, and Richmond and Hounslow, continued until the end of the century.

Lampton . . .

23. Left: The Black Horse Public House, Lampton Road, 1903. This inn was known to have been in existence by 1759. Up to 1925, there was a White Horse Public House nearby, and this is thought to be the reason for the building being covered with advertisements, to entice custom away from the rival establishment. The Black Horse was rebuilt in 1926, and the inn sign was painted by Lynwood Palmer, a well known painter of race horses.

24. Left: The Elms, Lampton Road, Hounslow, c. 1893. This farm lay back from the road, opposite The Lawn. It had been known earlier as "Old Sally Roger's Farm." At the end of the last century it was lived in by Mr. Alfred Platt, founder of Platts' Stores. The house was demolished at the beginning of this century, and Elmsworth Avenue, Avonwick Road, and Sunnycroft Road were built on the site.

The Bath Road to Cranford . . .

25. Left: Hounslow Barracks Station, renamed Hounslow West in 1925, opened on 21st July 1884. Route no. 82 bus service commenced in 1912, and ran from the Heston Hounslow Station, renamed Hounslow Central in 1925, to Staines. The photograph, taken around the period of the First World War, shows a London General Omnibus Company's "B" type bus, built in 1911, outside the station. Hounslow West Station was rebuilt in 1931 at a cost of £25,000.

26. Left: The Traveller's Friend Public House, c. 1930, shortly after it was rebuilt, showing the junction of the Great South West Road and the Great West Road. This junction is now known as Henley's Roundabout. The Traveller's Friend is listed in 1813, as a new built public house, with excellent stabling, and small garden.

The Great West Road was first mooted at the beginning of this century, and in 1914, the Great West Road Bill was passed by Parliament. For $5\frac{1}{2}$ years, during, and immediately after the First World War, nothing happened other than the acquisition of land. Work commenced from Syon Lane to the Bath Road in May 1920, and was completed in October 1923. The completed road from Gunnersbury to the Bath Road, and the Great South West Road extension to Bedfont, was opened on the 30th May 1925 by H.M. King George V and Queen Mary.

27. Left: The Berkeley Arms and Cranford Bridge Inn c.1914. This inn was situated on the Bath Road near to Cranford Bridge on the Harlington side. It was basically an 18th century coaching inn, but parts were said to date back to Tudor times. For about 60 years it was run by the Temple family until the beginning of this century. In January 1932 it was demolished to make way for road widening, and in the same year the present Berkeley Arms opened at the junction of The Avenue with the Bath Road.

28. Top right: Greenbank's Forge, Cranford, at the end of the 19th century. It was situated on the south side of the Bath Road, next to Cranford Bridge. The building still stands, although the brickwork has now been covered with cement. The forge was worked by Mr. George Greenbank and his two sons.

29. Bottom right: Cranford School and its pupils at the end of the last century. The school was situated on the Bath Road opposite the junction with Cranford High Street. It was built in 1883 and enlarged in 1887 at a cost of £1,400, which was raised by subscription. A class room was added in 1888 making accommodation for 166 children. The average attendance was 100 boys and girls and 50 infants. The school was in use until 1937, when Cranford Infants and Junior School opened in Berkeley Avenue. The Rev. Maurice Child then had a small temporary church built in the school grounds, called Holy Angels. This building was destroyed by fire in 1941 and rebuilt. It caught fire again in 1969 and was replaced by the present church in the High Street.

30. Far left: Cranford Post Office, 1895. This was situated on the Bath Road near to the junction with Cranford High Street. In the doorway can be seen Mr. William Leake, Postmaster, with the village postman, Bill Scarlet, who served Cranford for 30 years and then spent 10 years at Hounslow, before retiring in 1929. Mr. Leake was appointed sub-postmaster in October 1865 at a salary of £14. 8. od. per annum. The post office was then situated opposite the building shown in the photograph. In 1895 Mr. Leake had a new shop built for himself. As postmaster he was responsible for telegraphic and parcel delivery. The shop was also a grocers, bakers, and corn merchants. Mr. Leake died in 1908 and was succeeded by his wife, followed by his brother and then his daughter. In 1961 the post office moved to new premises in Cranford High Street, in order to make way for the widening of the Bath Road.

31. Centre: The village lock up, Cranford High Street, c.1890. The lock up was built c.1838 and is the last remaining cage within the Metropolitan Police area. It was used to house offenders prior to their appearance before the magistrates. The identity of the man in the photograph is not known, but the woman is Mrs. Brent, who used to do the washing for the Morland family at Sheepcotehaugh.

32. Top left: William Wyatt outside his butcher's shop in Cranford High Street, c.1890. This shop was situated near to the village lock up. Mr. Wyatt is listed as a butcher in the village as early as 1862, but his name had disappeared by 1899, although in that year the name of Mrs. Caroline Wyatt appears. He was known in the village as "Suetty".

33. Bottom left: Sheepcotehaugh, Cranford High Street, at the close of the last century. The house was demolished in 1969. Sheepcote Close was built on the site. At the beginning of the 19th century Sheepcotehaugh was three shepherds' cottages surrounded by a haugh or hedge. These were purchased in 1853 by Mr. Frederick H. Morland, a west-end tailor, who altered them into one house and called it Sheepcotehaugh. He lived there with his son Henry, daughter Emma, and her two sisters. Henry gave the plot of land on which the War Memorial Hall was built. Miss Emma died in 1935 aged 96 years.

Cranford Park . . .

34. Left: The Lodge to Cranford Park at the end of the last century. This building was at the junction of Church Road and Watersplash Lane. It was last lived in as a home in 1928, and was demolished during the Second World War. At the time of the photograph it was lived in by the gardener, Will Ausley and his wife, who is probably the woman standing in the doorway. Two carved stones can be seen on the wall of the house facing the road. On one was carved an Earl's coronet and on the other a mitre. On the drive side of the lodge was the coat-of-arms of the Berkeley family.

35. Left: The Rectory, Cranford, c.1890. This building stood just inside the lodge gates to Cranford Park, near to the junction of Church Road with Watersplash Lane. The Rectory still stands although the lodge and gates have gone. It is now used as a motorway maintenance office for the M4 Motorway, and is situated near to the roundabout on the Parkway, by the Cranford exit from the motorway. The east wing was originally a timber framed building of the 17th century, but was refaced with bricks and extended in the 18th century.

It was first used as a rectory in 1774, and continued to be used for that purpose until 1938, when the Rector moved to a house in Cranford High Street. During the Second World War it was used by the R.A.F. In the photograph can be seen the Rector, The Rev. J. F. L. Lee, and possibly members of his family.

36. Left: Cranford House, Cranford Park, c.1890, situated close to St. Dunstan's Church. Cranford Manor was owned by the Berkeley family from 1618-1918. In 1932 it was purchased by the local authority as a public open space. The house was either enlarged or rebuilt by the third Earl of Berkeley in 1722 and was extended to the south in 1792. After 1916 it remained empty, becoming more and more derelict, until it was demolished in 1945.

37. Left: St. Dunstan's Church, Cranford, c.1900-1910. The church is situated in Cranford Park and was then close to Cranford House. The chancel and lower part of the tower are portions of the original church, built in the 15th century. The tower now has three separate layers, the top being 17th century. The nave was destroyed by fire in 1710, and rebuilt by Lady Elizabeth Berkeley in 1716. Inside the church are many memorials to the Berkeley family, including a fine tomb to Elizabeth Berkeley, who died in 1635, and acquired Cranford Manor for the family. Opposite her tomb is the one to Sir Roger Aston, who died in 1612, and was the previous owner of the manor.

38. Top left: The Queen's Head Inn, Cranford, c.1890. This building stood in Cranford High Street at the junction with Cranford Lane, and was pulled down in 1931, when the present building was erected. The inn in the photograph dated back to the 17th century, having had a spirit licence from 1604.

39. Bottom left: Heston Airport, Cranford Lane, 1930, showing aircraft lined up for the start of The King's Cup Air Race. This event was attended by T.R.H. The Duke and Duchess of York, later H.M. King George VI and Queen Elizabeth. At the top of the photograph from left to right can be seen Cranford Lane. Heston Airport opened in July 1929 as a private venture. In 1937 it was purchased by the government and there were plans to develop it as the principal civil airport in the country. This involved buying up much of the surrounding land and the village of Cranford. The Second World War stopped the development and for the period of the war the airport was used by the R.A.F. In 1946 Heathrow was developed as the main airport of this country and Heston ceased to be an airport. Today the perimeter of the airport has been built upon. In 1938 the Prime Minister, Mr. Neville Chamberlain, landed at Heston after a meeting in Germany with Hitler. This was the occasion when he was photographed waving the famous piece of white paper and stating that he had brought peace in our time.

40. Centre: Heston House at the beginning of this century. This house stood at the junction of Cranford Lane with Vicarage Farm Road. The house dated from 1680 but was refronted in 1783. It had many owners and at the end of the 18th century Sir Joseph Banks had a mortgage on it. Thomas Fraser, Middlesex Magistrate, and later Lord Lovat lived there at the beginning of the 19th century. From 1827-1862 it was rented by the London parish of St. Giles as a home for poor children and from 1896-1911 was a boarding school for young gentlemen. The last owner from 1911-1937 was Mr. W. H. Fenton, J.P. Mr. Fenton is remembered as a collector of Hounslow swords. In 1932 one of his swords was presented to H.R.H. The Duke of Gloucester on the occasion of the Charter of the Borough of Heston and Isleworth. Following Mr. Fenton's death in 1937 the house was demolished.

41. Left: Heston Hall c.1910-1920. This house stood in Vicarage Farm Road on the site of the present United Reformed Church. The house was 18th century and owned from the mid 18th century until 1927 by the Hogarth family. Col. J. R. Hogarth was a Heston Councillor on the first Middlesex County Council in 1888. After his death in 1899 the house and farm was let to Arthur Nicholas, market gardener until it was demolished in 1927. In 1931 Heston Congregational Church was built on the site. This recently changed its name to The United Reformed Church.

Heston Village . . .

42. Far left: The Bakery, New Heston Road, pre 1890. It was then owned by a family called Stracey. In 1905 it was purchased by J. Harle Ltd., who ran it until it closed on Christmas Eve 1968, and the shop sold for demolition. In the early 1970's new houses were built on the site. The building was thought to be 200 years old and had always been used as a bakery.

43. Top left: New Heston Road, c.1910. The shop with the first floor overhang, seen behind the two girls, was owned by Mr. Dicky Wingrove, and later by Benham, the basket maker. The Co-operative store now stands on the site. To the left of the girls was a field, which lead to the village smithy, owned by George Gilbert, who also farmed the surrounding land, which is now Walnut Tree Road.

44. Bottom left: Highclere was situated on the Heston Road, at the rear of the present Heron Garage. It was lived in during the 17th century by Elizabeth, daughter of Oliver. Cromwell. In the 1920s when this photograph was taken, it was a hotel. The house was demolished in 1935.

45. Top left: Mr. Edward Paine, post-master of Heston, c.1920. The building was demolished about 1924 and the present post office was built, by Platt's stores. The Paine family were connected with Heston post office from the mid 19th century. His father, Edwin Paine, was postmaster until his death in 1869, and was succeeded by his mother, Jane. On her retirement in 1903 she was succeeded by Edward, who died in 1928.

46. Bottom left: Heston Fire Station built in 1895 on the Heston Road in the corner of Heston Infants School playground. The foreman from 1899 until he retired in 1920 was Mr. Richard Wingrove, greengrocer. He may have held the position from the opening in 1895, and is possibly the gentleman in the photograph. Fire practice was held in the recreation ground where Heston Comprehensive School now stands, and when there was a fire, the horse grazing in the field had to be caught and harnessed to the fire cart. The horse always went up Heston Road and along Church Road, before he could be persuaded to turn in the direction of the fire. The fire station closed in 1926 and it was used by Heston Infants School from that date, apart for one year 1932/1933, when it was used as Heston Public Library prior to the opening of the temporary library in New Heston Road. The building is now used as a store for Heston Infants School.

Jersey Road to Spring Grove . . .

47. Right: The Hole in the Wall, Jersey Road c.1920-1930. This is a gate in the wall of the Osterley Estate, and was combined with a stile, which has now disappeared. Once inside the Osterley Estate one can walk across the fields to Osterley House, Norwood Green, or Heston Church.

48. Far right: St. Mary's Church, Spring Grove, 1870. The church was built 1852-1856 to serve the new Victorian estate of Spring Grove, and was the personal gift of the developer, Henry Daniel Davies, at a cost of £15,000. The estate was never completed because Davies lost his money in an unwise Italian investment. Note the rough, stony surface of Osterley Road.

To HESTON   To WYKE GREEN

SPRING GROVE CHURCH 1870

49. Left: London Road, Isleworth looking east, c.1897. On the left, a cart laden with baskets is leaving Star Road. The Star Public House stands on the east corner.

50. Left: Trams passing the Hounslow Depot in the London Road. The London United Tramway Co. built the 10 track depot with a substation alongside in 1901, for the electric trams between Kew Bridge and Hounslow, which commenced in July of that year. They were an instant success with the hundreds of employees of Pear's soap factory, who forsook the trains for the trams. The first car of the day ran at 4 a.m.; the last tram at 2 a.m. next morning.

51. Left: Pear's Fountain, Spring Grove. View looking towards Hounslow from the junction of Spring Grove Road with the London Road. The fountain was presented to the inhabitants of Heston and Isleworth by Andrew Pears, J.P., C.A. in 1899. Lady Jersey performed the opening ceremony which consisted of turning on the water and taking the first drink from the fountain. She spoke of the generosity of Mr. Pears in not only thinking of the upper classes, but of the passers-by who would use the fountain and go away refreshed, with their thoughts full of the kind and generous spirit of Mr. Pear's water. The fountain was removed in the 1930s as it had become an obstruction to traffic.

52. Left: The Diamond Jubilee procession, London Road, Isleworth, 1897, showing the Dragoons passing by Isleworth Station. There were fields by the station towards St. John's Road. A horse is standing in College Road on the right.

53. Left: Isleworth Station Staff 1880-1881. Note the advertisements and the bookstall behind the group. The two boys are possibly newspaper sellers.

54. Left: Isleworth Railway Station, looking east, 1904. The caption reads 'The 3.44 Down'. The station was opened in 1849 and was the terminus of the loop line of the London and South Western Railway. It was called Smallberry Green. In 1850 the line was extended to Hounslow and the station renamed Isleworth.

55. Left: Floods in London Road, Isleworth, on June 19th 1914, after a severe storm in which many houses in the area were struck by lightning. The steep dip under the bridge and the inadequate drainage always resulted in flooding after heavy rain. The entrance to Pears' Soap Works is on the left.

56. Left: Busch Corner, Iselworth, c.1905, looking east towards Brentford. The stall on the left, marked 'Spratt and Sons, Isleworth', stands outside fields on which the Green School was built in 1906. The Twickenham Road branches off to the right, by the lady with the perambulator. The tram wires show the direction. Syon Lodge can be seen in the distance on the right. Spur Road was not then in existence.

57. Left: Syon Hill Farm, c.1890. It was known as Moore's Farm, and stood on the site of Gillette's factory. The caption of the photograph reads 'Getting ready for market loading produce'.

58. Left: Isleworth Fire Brigade with their new motor fire engine outside the fire station on the Twickenham Road, opposite Gumley House, c.1904. This fire station was used until the present station on the London Road opened in 1937. On the left of the picture is Mr. J. W. G. Hubbard, a member for 47 years, who retired as Second Officer in 1939. The engine was previously housed under the end portion of Isleworth Blue School in the square.

59. Left: Thomas Love, Isleworth Parish Beadle, c.1870, who held the office of Beadle until his death. He was a tall, commanding figure, dressed in gold-lace braided waistcoat and coat, knee breeches, and decorated wand of office. His office included coroner's officer, town crier, and a leading figure in the ceremony of Beating the Bounds.

"A Bit of Old Isleworth", South Street 1903

Isleworth Village . . .

60. Left: South Street, c.1903. The street was very narrow with shops on both sides. On the left hand side of the photograph are: the forge owned by F. Sadler, whose sign reads "Cycles and General Repairs; shoeing and general repairs of all kinds neatly executed"; at no. 78. R. Watts, hairdresser, "stop here for an easy shave". No. 74, the shop with the canopy, was owned by Balch, the butcher. It was a common sight to see flocks of sheep driven through South Street to the slaughter house at the rear of the shop. On the right side of the photograph at the corner of Algar Road, can be seen Taylor & Sons, ironmongers, who opened an oil and colour shop in 1885. The shop nearest to the camera, on the right, has the sign "Gold Flake 10 for 3d."

61. Top right: Upper Square, Isleworth, at the end of the 19th century. The drinking fountain was erected in 1870 in memory of the Rev. Henry Glossop, vicar of Isleworth, 1822-1855. The photograph shows on the left, W. Hillier, (described as a baker in the Middx. Chron. directory 1899) at no. 2; J. Lee, fishmonger, at no. 3; Mrs. Vernon at no. 4, called, 'shopkeeper'. Opposite was E. D. Roe at nos. 7 and 8, grocer and post office. The carts are travelling towards the Swan Street junction.

62. Bottom right: The Blue School and The Northumberland Arms, Lower Square, at the beginning of this century. Kidd's Granary Store can be seen in the background. The Blue School was erected in 1841, the 18th century building being impractical. The school occupied the upper storey, the ground floor being used as a playground. The Northumberland Arms was built early in the 19th century, and was the Court Leet for the Dukes of Northumberland. The quarterly rents were paid there, followed by a meal. The Parish Beadle and Constable stood on duty outside the main entrance.

63. Top left: Samuel Kidd and Co. Ltd., Isleworth Flour Mills. In 1894 it was remodelled from a stone-mill into a roller-mill, and was one of the most modern mills in the London area. The barges came under the road bridge into the mill basin to load and unload.

64. Bottom left: Church Street looking east towards the church, early this century. The photograph was taken from the mill bridge, showing the vicarage railings on the left, the house being hidden by the trees. The cottages on the left stood on "Frog Hill".

65. Right: Aerial view of the river frontage at Isleworth, 1926. The West Middlesex Hospital is at the top left of the photograph; the Duke of Northumberland's River crosses from left to right, entering the Thames by Tolson's Almshouses. The parish church stands on the far right by the River Thames. Church Street leads from the right to Kidd's Mill (in the centre) which dominated the area. On the south side of the street is Holland House, with two bay windows and a fine garden leading down to the river. Lower Square can be seen in the corner, bottom left, with shops around one side by the Northumberland Arms, with the no. 37 buses waiting in the forecourt. The Blue School (1841 building) is at the bottom left of the photograph, with the North Street School seen midway along the left hand edge.

66. Left: The interior of All Saint's Church, Isleworth, prior to the alterations of 1866-1867. The photograph is taken looking towards the east, showing the 1706 nave with box pews on either side of the aisle, with the servants' pews in the centre facing the triple-decker pulpit. Monuments to Sir Orlando Gee, and Mrs. Anne Tolson, can be seen to the right of the pulpit.

67. Left: The interior of All Saint's Church, Isleworth, after the alterations of 1866-1867. The chancel was added in the Gothic style, and paid for mainly by the Farnell family, who owned Isleworth Brewery. The stonework of the reredos and the decoration in the chancel were in memory of John Farnell. The east end shows the Ten Commandments, the Creed, and the Lord's Prayer, mounted on the chancel arch. This building was gutted by fire in 1943; started by the two youths who had earlier fired Holy Trinity Church, Hounslow.

ALL SAINTS CHURCH, ISLEWORTH.

68. Right: 'Isleworth when the tide is low', 1905. School children are seen enjoying the delights of the river at low tide. The photograph shows the river bank, and the barges moored behind the cottages in Church Street. The sundial can be seen on the wall of the church.

69. Right: The London Apprentice, 1905, viewed from the Isleworth Ait. Finn's boathouse and boatbuilding business stood at Isleworth Dock, in front of the church. The sign of the London Apprentice stated "Tea Parties, Chops and Steaks".

70. Below: The start of the Isleworth Skiff Marathon, August 21st 1909, showing the Tradesmen's Section. This was the inaugural race of the marathon which followed the course from Isleworth to Putney Bridge and back. It was started as a long distance race for double sculling crews with two sections—Amateur crews were awarded the Heldmann Cup and the Tradesmen's crews received an award from Messrs. E. & J. Beck.